THE NEED TO KNOW LIBRARY™

EVERYTHING YOU NEED TO KNOW ABOUT ANGER MANAGEMENT

CORONA BREZINA

Rosen YA™
New York

Published in 2019 by The Rosen Publishing Group, Inc.
29 East 21st Street, New York, NY 10010

First Edition

Library of Congress Cataloging-in-Publication Data

Names: Brezina, Corona, author.
Title: Everything you need to know about anger management / Corona Brezina.
Description: Rosen Publishing : New York, 2019 | Series: The need to know library | Audience: Grades 7–12. | Includes bibliographical references and index.
Identifiers: LCCN 2018002660| ISBN 9781508183402 (library bound) | ISBN 9781508183396 (pbk.)
Subjects: LCSH: Anger—Juvenile literature.
Classification: LCC BF575.A5 B748 2018 | DDC 155.5/1247—dc23
LC record available at https://lccn.loc.gov/2018002660

Manufactured in the United States of America

CONTENTS

INTRODUCTION

On July 5, 2017, an airline passenger's rage and disruptive behavior led to the delay of a plane leaving Atlanta, Georgia, bound for Chicago, Illinois. The incident began when a woman reportedly refused to bring her seat up from the reclining position as the plane began taxiing. When a flight attendant approached her, the passenger became combative, getting up to follow her and screaming profanities. Meanwhile, the woman's small dog ran loose in the aisle. The incident led to the plane turning around and the passenger being removed from the flight, causing a four-hour delay.

Reports about the effects of out-of-control anger aren't uncommon in the news. The media frequently describes various extreme outbursts of air rage and road rage. Surveys provide statistics about people getting angry at work, at school, and in public places. Commentators debate whether society as a whole is getting angrier.

Anger itself is a perfectly normal emotion to feel. The problem is when people let their anger take control of them, resulting in outbursts, resentment, and all kinds of other destructive behavior.

If you've observed the effects of problem anger, you're not alone. According to a British survey by the Mental Health Foundation, nearly a third of respondents said that they had a close friend or family member with

Anger management classes can help people learn healthier ways of expressing anger, such as using problem-solving skills rather than responding with aggression.

anger management problems. One in five reported that they'd ended a friendship or relationship because of anger issues. Although only about one in ten said that they had problems managing their own anger, nearly half admitted to having lost their temper at work at least once.

Out-of-control anger can be a serious problem that can affect many aspects of a person's life. It can be harmful to physical and mental health, it can hurt relationships, and people with anger management issues often receive less social support from family and friends.

For people exhibiting problem anger, extreme reactions to provocations can become an entrenched habit. Anger is an emotion, and aggression is a type of behavior. Some people automatically react to anger with aggression, but this is not a healthy response. It is possible to change, however, using anger management techniques. When channeled in healthy ways, anger can be a constructive force that can help people accomplish their goals.

If you are experiencing anger problems, there are resources and mental health professionals to help you learn healthy skills for managing anger. As a teen, you're at a point in your life when bad anger habits haven't yet become deeply established through years of reacting destructively. Learning effective anger management habits can help you improve many aspects of your life, from performance at school to personal relationships.

CHAPTER ONE

A PROBLEM WITH ANGER

Most people don't give much thought to anger in their daily lives. It's normal to feel angry on occasion, after all. Usually the feeling dissipates after the problem is resolved or the person moves on to other activities. But some people can't control their anger, and it can affect the quality of their own lives and the lives of their friends, family members, and coworkers. Anger can be toxic—it can poison healthy trust and communication in personal and professional relationships. In extreme scenarios, it can cause a person's life to spiral out of control. However, it is possible to manage your anger. The first step is acknowledging the problem and taking steps to understand anger.

UNDERSTANDING ANGER

Anger is one of the most basic human emotions, along with happiness, sadness, and fear. Anger is an intense emotional reaction to a provocation, such as an action or comment by another person or a disturbing incident. Sometimes, simply thinking about unpleasant topics can be enough to make someone angry.

Anger spurs physical as well as mental reactions. A common way to describe a person who is angry is to say that that person's "blood is up." That idiom does reflect how your heart rate and blood pressure rises when you feel angry. Your muscles may tense and you may clench your fists without consciously deciding to do so. Anger can trigger many different feelings depending on the individual and circumstances. A burst of anger could make one person feel energized and confident, while it could leave someone else feeling bitter and depressed.

Other people's words and actions are one of the most common triggers for anger.

Likewise, there are many different ways of expressing anger. Some people are open about their angry feelings, conveying them through words or actions. This can lead to aggression and even violent confrontations. Such out-of-control behavior is what most people think of when they think of someone having a problem with anger. But some other ways of dealing with anger can also have negative consequences. Some people suppress their anger by bottling it up. Others may repress their anger by denying even to themselves that they're feeling angry.

Anger management experts sometimes categorize the different ways that people deal with their anger. For example, in his book *Letting Go of Anger: The Eleven Most Common Anger Styles and What to Do About Them*, psychotherapist and author Ronald T. Potter-Efron describes different anger styles. These include explosive anger styles, such as exploding into rage or intimidating others with anger, and chronic anger styles, such as hostility or holding a grudge. These behaviors are unmistakable—you don't have to be an expert to recognize them.

Potter-Efron also discusses masked anger styles, in which people hide their anger from themselves or others. People who use what he calls "sneaky anger," for example, behave passive-aggressively instead of openly showing their anger. They may sabotage plans that they make with others or fail to fulfill commitments. People sometimes turn their anger inward, blaming themselves for bad situations or resorting to self-destructive behavior.

Perception of anger can vary depending on the situation. You might think that you expressed reasonable anger, but to an observer, it might look like you'd lost control. Sometimes one member of a family or group of friends feels that having a hot temper is no big deal, but it can make people around that person feel uncomfortable and even poison personal relationships.

When thinking about how you or the people around you handle anger, keep in mind that some demonstrations of anger can be more subtle than tantrums or visible resentment.

CONSTRUCTIVE AND DESTRUCTIVE ANGER

Anger in itself is neither good nor bad. It's completely normal to get angry about people, events, and problems. In most cases, anger isn't unhealthy. Most people are able to express their anger appropriately, without allowing emotions to overrule common sense and socially acceptable behavior in a situation.

Anger evolved to allow humans to react aggressively to a physical threat, such as an attack by a predator. The body's responses—increased heart rate, faster breathing, a surge of energy—occur so that people are prepared physically to defend themselves. In modern society, however, most situations that trigger anger don't require a physically aggressive reaction.

Nonetheless, when channeled toward a specific purpose, anger can be constructive. The energy produced by anger can be a powerful motivator. Anger can provoke someone into action—perhaps to fix something, finish a project, or solve a problem. In some cases, anger may prompt a person to make major changes in her life. Getting angry can reveal insights, leading someone to realize she might be happier if she looked for a new job, for example, or recognize a need for self-improvement. Anger can even be good for relationships. Expressing rather than bottling up anger can lead to improved communication, as long as both partners work toward a solution to the root problems causing the anger.

More broadly, widespread anger over injustice has been a motivating factor in social movements throughout history. Activists who rally for causes such as women's rights, civil rights, and protecting the environ-

Widespread anger over social injustice can lead to organized protest movements that challenge discriminatory policies or practices and focus public attention on the issue.

ment are spurred on by anger over discrimination and abuses of power.

When people lose control of their anger, however, it can become destructive. If you exhibit toxic anger, it can affect your physical health, the well-being of people around you, relationships, schoolwork, and employment

TEENS AND ANGER ISSUES

There's a common notion that people get angrier as they get older, but the opposite is actually true. People are generally the most angry during their teenage years and in their early twenties. Adolescence is a period of major life changes. Teenagers are in the process of maturing physically and psychologically. They're taking on more responsibilities, preparing for independence, and experimenting with different ways to express their identities. Adolescence brings about many transformations and milestones that are exciting but that also cause pressure and stress. At the same time, teenagers lack the life experience that can provide reassurance that everything will turn out okay.

It's natural for teenagers to experience mood swings and feel buffeted by strong emotions, including anger, during this turbulent period of life. Adolescents can benefit from examining their feelings and learning healthy ways to express emotions. Forming good habits for managing anger and other emotions during your teenage years can be crucial in establishing long-term patterns of constructive anger management.

prospects. Chronic or explosive anger drains energy and can lead to unhealthy behaviors. An inability to control your temper can alienate romantic partners, friends, coworkers, and employers. Teens can get in trouble in school when anger leads to fights and other forms of rebellion. Well-qualified workers can have their careers derailed by anger management problems, which can range from passive counterproductive behavior to aggressive or even violent outbursts.

THE HABIT OF ANGER

When someone gets angry, that person reacts or responds to a provocation. Psychologists sometimes differentiate between the terms "react" and "respond," even though most people consider them interchangeable. A reaction is instantaneous, instinctive, and emotional. If you are angered by some bad news and slam your fist against your desk, that's a reaction. A reaction takes only short-term considerations into account—the reaction of lashing out physically won't help resolve the cause of the anger. A response, by contrast, involves thought as well as emotion. When you respond to the source of your anger, you take into consideration the consequences and the appropriateness of your immediate actions. This may involve restraining a reaction that could just make the situation worse. Anger management experts often encourage people to respond to anger instead of merely reacting.

Deciding to address problem anger requires self-reflection and a long-term commitment to changing one's thoughts and actions.

Often, even when people recognize that they have a problem with anger, they still can't control it. For many people, anger management requires rejecting an automatic reaction to anger in favor of a more measured response. It can also mean letting go of other unhealthy ways of handling anger, such as holding grudges, suppressing anger, or engaging in passive-aggressive behavior.

People can get stuck in a pattern of reacting a certain way when they're angry. In this sense, anger can be viewed as a habit. Some habits are good, such as studying regularly or getting plenty of exercise; others, such as substance abuse or overspending, are bad. People can break their bad anger habits and replace them with constructive means of dealing with anger.

As with quitting any bad habit, dealing with problem anger isn't a quick or easy undertaking. The process begins with self-reflection. Learning to manage an anger problem requires a reassessment of deep-seated assumptions about anger. For example, perhaps you feel that your angry reactions are impossible to control or that expressing your anger aggressively makes you seem more powerful. Handling anger constructively will always be hardest during stressful times. "Relapses" may occur, but that's to be expected. Anger management is an ongoing process, so you shouldn't expect to change (yourself or anyone else) overnight.

MYTHS AND FACTS

MYTH: Anger is bad.

FACT: Anger is a natural, healthy emotion. People's response to anger, not the emotion itself, determines whether it has a positive or negative effect on their lives. Anger can be constructive when channeled into positive action or destructive when expressed as aggressive outbursts or resentment or bottled up and repressed.

MYTH: Anger management doesn't work because anger isn't something that can be controlled.

FACT: You may not be able to prevent feelings of anger, but you can control how you express that anger. Dealing with anger is a learned response that becomes a habit. It's possible to change by learning healthy responses that can replace harmful angry reactions.

MYTH: If I don't let out my anger, I might explode.

FACT: This myth is based on the idea that unexpressed anger can build up over time, creating pressure that needs to be released. However, most experts agree that venting through tirades or outbursts isn't healthy. A failure to restrain outbursts of anger actually leads to a pattern of more anger in the future. (Venting one's frustration to a sympathetic friend, by contrast, can be a healthy alternative to suppressing anger.)

CHAPTER TWO

TRIGGERS, OUTBURSTS, AND OVERREACTIONS

Anger management isn't about totally suppressing anger—for most people, never getting angry is impossible. Rather, anger management aims to give people the tools to deal with anger in healthier ways. Problem anger can hurt people's quality of life and leave them feeling as if they're unable to control their own behavior. Recognizing the triggers that provoke angry reactions and understanding the root causes of anger can help you resolve to make life changes in order to address anger problems.

SOURCES OF ANGER

Everybody has their own specific anger triggers—provocations that are sure to make them angry. These are often people or situations, such as an unexpected frustration or disappointment. Triggers may be personal, such as a perceived slight, insult, or instance of unfairness. They provoke anger whether they are meant to hurt—when a classmate insults your clothing, for

If you find that you're easily angered by minor inconveniences, ask yourself if you tend to exaggerate the negative aspects of everyday situations.

example—or are unintentional, such as when someone accidentally spills a drink on your belongings. You'll probably feel angry if you get a bad grade on a school assignment, if you're falsely blamed for something, or if a friend forgets a lunch date.

Other triggers, such as annoyances of everyday life, are impersonal occurrences. People get angry at bad drivers, lost packages in the mail, incompetent coworkers, long lines, computer glitches, or poor customer service. Such situations are beyond your control, but they provoke feelings of anger anyway.

Keeping an anger log, with information such as provocations, reactions, and outcomes to the situation, can help you plan how to better manage your anger.

Triggers don't have to be immediate events, either. People get angry at news stories about injustices or simply by summoning up a memory of an old enemy. Negative thought patterns can worsen anger problems, as well. These include, for example, predicting that the worst outcome will occur in any situation or assuming that someone doesn't like you even if you have no reason to think that.

It's possible to learn to identify situations in which you are likely to have an excessive reaction. Some people bottle up their anger until they get home, then

ROAD RAGE

Road rage is defined by the AAA Foundation for Traffic Safety as "any unsafe driving maneuver performed deliberately and with ill intention or disregard for safety." In such a scenario, a single driver's anger management issues could have dangerous consequences for everyone on the road. Road rage incidents range from aggressive driving tactics, such as tailgating or running red lights, to recklessness and even assault, such as by ramming another vehicle or getting out to physically confront another driver.

Driving can be a stressful and frustrating experience, especially when it involves factors such as bad weather, heavy traffic, construction, and unexpected delays. People on the road are often in a rush to get to their destination, and bad behavior by other drivers can seem infuriating. Young men are the most common road rage offenders, but many people who are usually polite and cautious engage in reckless moves behind the wheel. To keep yourself from becoming a road rage victim, drive courteously and try to put distance between yourself and aggressive drivers. If you're tempted to retaliate or communicate your own frustration through your driving, remind yourself of the potential consequences of a car crash and practice anger management techniques to keep your cool.

vent at the slightest irritation. Others tend to get angry in crowded public places or in traffic, where the stress of handling a chaotic situation can spill over into rage. People may also display problem anger in the workplace or in social settings, turning interactions into confrontations.

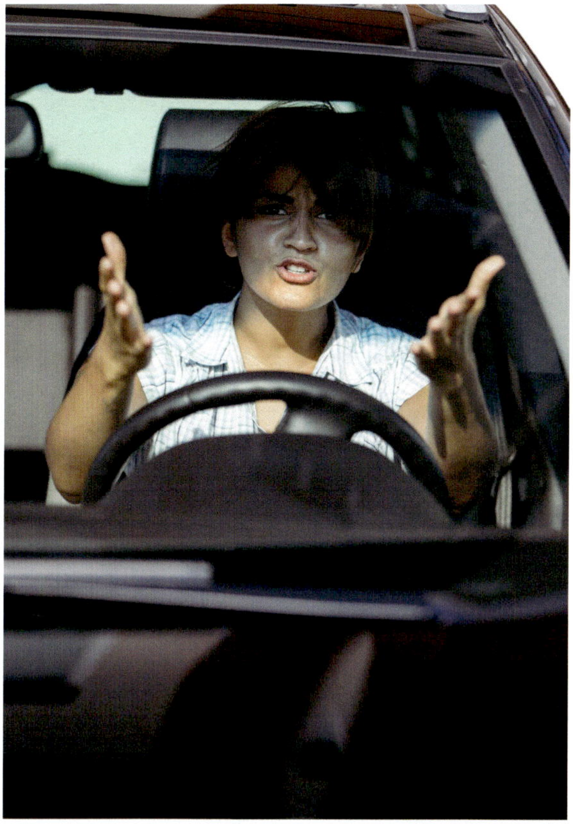

A driver who is feeling stressed or impatient may react aggressively and dangerously at slight provocations.

Anger management experts often recommend keeping a journal or log of anger triggers. The purpose of this log is more to identify patterns of behavior than engage in self-reflection. It generally includes the place and time of each "anger event" along with a brief description. Additional information, such as physical feelings or a ranking of the intensity of your anger, can also be helpful. After tracking instances of anger for a period of time, certain patterns will emerge. Identifying the circumstances most likely to provoke anger can help you to devise strategies to prevent such situations and prepare responses for triggers that are likely to occur in the future.

RECOGNIZING ANGER ISSUES

Usually, people with anger management issues don't need to ask whether they have a problem with anger. Over-the-top anger can get kids into trouble in school and even with the law. If anger leads to physical violence, it's definitely a problem. Frequent arguments, reckless behavior because of anger, and people telling you that you have an issue with anger are clear indications that you need to learn to manage your anger. A person with anger problems can even feel frightened by his or her own anger spinning out of control.

Demonstrations of toxic anger are often frequent and intense. A reaction to a provocation can range from irritation to anger to rage. Occurrences can be either episodic—happening only occasionally—or chronic, meaning that they take place at least on a daily basis. Chronic anger or chronic rage qualifies as a problem that affects a person's quality of life and should be managed. People with anger management problems often recognize that their reaction is out of proportion to the trigger. They know that they shouldn't blow up over a minor issue, but they can't control the irrational anger.

Normally, anger is an emotion that arises quickly and doesn't last for long. Holding on to anger can be unhealthy, whether it's stewing over an insult for hours or holding a grudge for years.

The most extreme form of anger is rage—explosive anger in which someone completely loses control of their behavior. People experiencing rage often act destructively and are incapable of listening to reason. Sometimes, they report afterward that they felt like they had transformed into a different person during an episode of rage.

Uncontrolled anger and rage are the best-known forms of toxic anger, but unexpressed anger can also be destructive. Passive-aggressive behavior and anger turned inward can affect your well-being and relationships with others. If you observe these tendencies in yourself, try to identify the triggers that are the root causes of your anger. This can help you plan strategies to confront such issues directly in healthy ways, rather than creating frustration for yourself and others by acting out anger indirectly.

ROOT CAUSES OF ANGER

We all have our own unique circumstances that contribute to how we experience anger. People react to different triggers and express their anger in different ways. Have you ever found yourself seething over an issue that doesn't bother anybody else around you or watched someone else blow up over what seems to you a minor issue? At the root of many anger management issues is a low threshold for frustration—some people simply cannot tolerate even minor annoyances.

There are a broad range of factors that determine people's angry reactions. According to the American Psychological Association, research has shown that some people are biologically predisposed toward having a hot temper. Anger is one of the traits that make up temperament, which is a core part of an individual's personality. Even from an early age, some children are naturally more prickly and quick to anger than others.

Upbringing and family life also affect how people react to triggers and display their anger. Some kids live in angry homes where family members tend to communicate poorly and fail to resolve conflicts in a healthy manner. Children take this behavior as a model and are at risk of developing anger management problems as they grow up.

Social and cultural factors also influence how people handle anger. Kids see examples of different ways of managing anger from peers and adult authority figures such as teachers and clergy. They also absorb lessons from media, such as movies, television, books, video games, and the internet. Often, society sends mixed messages about appropriate ways of dealing with anger. Adults may urge kids to act one way but set a different example with their own behavior. Some conventional wisdom claims that anger is a destructive force that should be repressed. An alternate take on anger insists that it's a natural instinct that's impossible to control.

For boys, the messages can be particularly contradictory. Boys are often raised to avoid behaviors that are seen as feminine, such as crying or openly expressing emotions, while they are encouraged to be aggressive. Some boys feel pushed toward expressing anger because it is seen as more manly, even when it runs contrary to their nature. They may express other underlying emotions, such as sadness, through angry reactions.

When boys are taught that crying is for girls, they may learn to express their sadness as rage instead.

Stress is another major factor in problem anger. The body reacts to stress with many of the same physical responses as it does to anger. Handling stress badly can turn minor irritations into triggers for anger.

Finally, anger management issues may be related to underlying physical or mental health conditions. In an extreme scenario, uncontrollable anger can be a consequence of a traumatic brain injury, such as when football players sustain repeated concussions. Other physical conditions that can affect mood and anger include hormone imbalances, chronic pain, low blood sugar, and lack of sleep. Mental health conditions that may involve outbursts of anger include depression, bipolar disorder, borderline personality disorder, post-traumatic stress disorder (PTSD), attention deficit/hyperactivity disorder (ADHD), and substance abuse. If you find yourself experiencing mental or physical symptoms in addition to anger management issues, ask a doctor if they could be related.

CHAPTER THREE

CALMING DOWN

Once a person recognizes that he has a problem with anger management and makes a decision to change, the next step is making a sincere commitment to the process. Undertaking a major behavioral adjustment isn't easy, and people tend to hold on to their patterns of angry reactions even when they recognize that anger is causing nothing but trouble. Deciding to change requires reexamining your assumptions about anger. For example, people might believe deep down that their anger is justified, that it's not really possible to control anger after all or that anger provides a source of strength in a conflict. It's important to reframe these assumptions: angry reactions are a problem regardless of the trigger, anger definitely can be controlled, and it takes greater strength of character to control anger than to let it control you.

Short-term anger management tactics can help you deal with situations in which you're seething in frustration or about to blow your fuse.

ADJUST YOUR THINKING

Outbursts of anger often occur as a result of built-up stress. Identifying the various causes of stress in your life can help you defuse anger.

One of the goals of anger management is to prevent an excessive reaction to a trigger. After you've identified your triggers, plan a strategy for handling anger in various scenarios. One smart tactic is avoidance. If you're liable to blow up when you're in a rush, for example, allow plenty of extra time in your schedule. Distraction can work, too. If you recognize symptoms of anger coming on, force yourself to focus your attention on something else. Restrain yourself from impulsive actions that you might later regret—it's unwise to send emails or texts in the heat of anger.

It's not possible or desirable to avoid all anger triggers, however. You should prepare a calm response to specific triggers that you can use as an alternative to an instinctive reaction. When provoked,

ANGER IN THE WORKPLACE

When you enter the world of work, your first job will give you the opportunity to establish a sound work ethic and learn how to be a good employee. Ideally, people would leave their anger issues outside the door and treat coworkers with respect and professionalism. But the workplace can be stressful, frustrating, and competitive, and provocations on the job can sometimes leave workers seething or fuming. Although anger may flare up publicly in a conflict, employees often demonstrate anger in more subtle ways. They may engage in counterproductive work behavior, such as taking longer than necessary to finish tasks or treating customers rudely. If you find yourself feeling angry in the workplace, resist the temptation to express it through poor work performance. Draw on anger management techniques if necessary. Establishing good work habits early on will be beneficial to your future career.

take a deep breath and do a reality check. Ask yourself: does the situation really warrant a drastic reaction? Anger management experts sometimes urge people to differentiate between events and causes. For example, if you're trying to concentrate and a group of people are distracting you by speaking loudly, you may automatically blame them for your inability to work. In reality, though, the people around you didn't intend any offense—the cause of your anger is your own perception of the situation. Likewise, inconveniences such as a bus arriving late or the wrong food order being delivered for lunch are merely events, and it's your reaction that makes you angry.

If your trigger is a perceived slight from another person, you might automatically view the situation as a conflict that you want to win. According to this mindset, backing down would demonstrate weakness. Instead of attempting to force a confrontation, however, try taking a deep breath and considering the situation from a different perspective. Rather than a conflict, approach it as a problem that requires solving. Being able to control anger is a strength, not a weakness, since uncontrolled anger is unlikely to be effective in achieving a solution. "Winning" by dominating the other person might make the situation worse. Instead, aim to resolve the problem.

RELAXATION SKILLS

Relaxation techniques are a tool that can help people calm down their mental and physical responses to anger. In psychological terms, relaxing doesn't mean getting comfortable during your spare time, although that's an important thing to do as well. Relaxation is the process of calming the physical and mental responses to provocation or stress.

Body awareness can help lessen the intensity of your emotions when you're angry. Are you experiencing tense muscles, tightness in your chest, and fast

By mastering relaxation techniques, you can train yourself to reduce the tension in your body that occurs during trigger situations and that leads to angry reactions.

breathing? Are you snarling or scowling? Physical messages from your body are linked to your emotions. Make an effort to unclench your muscles, starting with your face. Body awareness can help you recognize physical signs that are setting up an angry reaction. Some people use a process called progressive muscle relaxation to relieve tension related to stress or anxiety.

An important relaxation technique recommended by all anger management experts is deep breathing. Taking a slow breath before responding to a trigger can be useful as a delaying tactic, but the most effective

MANAGING ANGER ONLINE

The advent of the internet and social media has created far-reaching new ways for people to communicate, obtain information, and participate in shared activities. This connectivity has brought many benefits, but it also creates a setting in which people can exhibit bad behavior and vent anger. Online interactions lead to anger triggers of all kinds, from personal barbs on social media to news stories expressing objectionable political views. For many people, the automatic reaction is to post a hurtful comment that's immediately visible across the internet. They may express views and hurl insults that they'd never dare say to another person face to face. Online communication offers a lack of accountability, especially when opinions are anonymous. Even when a person's identity is known, that person is still removed from the consequences of angry outbursts—he or she doesn't have to watch someone else react with hurt or indignation.

It might sometimes seem like venting anger online is no big deal since it's so common. Nonetheless, online aggression is unhealthy and is generally an unproductive means of debating opposing viewpoints. Posting hateful comments doesn't give anyone involved a chance to deescalate a disagreement and reach a resolution. Online cruelty can have real-world consequences, too. Friends can be hurt by thoughtless comments on social media, and this can affect personal relationships. In extreme scenarios, online posts can be interpreted as threats by school authorities or even the police. If you're ever tempted to vent your anger on the internet or engage in a social media dispute, take a step back and consider the real impact of your words.

technique involves "belly breaths," those taken from the diaphragm all the way at the bottom of the lungs. Deep breathing can help clear the mind, reduce tension, and even reduce intense emotions. The technique may require some practice, but once you've mastered deep breathing, you can use it in situations in which you need to defuse angry reactions.

Some people use calming words to help manage anger. As you're taking a deep breath, mentally repeat a word or phrase, such as "relax" or "it's OK," that you've selected in advance.

Imagery is another relaxation technique that can help cool angry reactions. Imagery is the use of the

Whether anger is sparked by real-world hassles or online provocations, try not to overreact. Ask yourself if acting aggressively is really appropriate for the situation.

imagination to visualize a relaxing or positive scene, perhaps a beach or a garden full of flowers. The image you choose should be highly detailed, and you should focus on the sounds and smells as well as the visual elements. People sometimes imagine stepping through a door to make an easy transition to the relaxation scene. During times of tension, you can use this technique to briefly summon up a calming image that can help control intense emotions.

These techniques are most effective if you practice them in advance in a quiet setting to familiarize yourself with the processes rather than trying them out for the first time in the heat of anger. Even if you don't make an in-depth study of relaxation techniques, you can get in the habit of taking a deep breath or waiting a moment to reflect before responding to a trigger. This forces you to take time to focus on self-control instead of reacting impulsively.

DELIBERATE RESPONSES

At first, it won't be easy to respond in a controlled manner to a trigger rather than reacting instinctively. Try refocusing on your own feelings and responses rather than lashing out at the trigger. Instead of fuming over someone else's mistake that inconvenienced you, take a quick reality check. Ask yourself why the incident is bothering you so much.

If you know you can't control yourself, walk away from a conflict. People usually get over anger more

If your body is feeling tense because of anger, try doing jumping jacks or drinking something cold to physically distract your body.

quickly if they remove themselves from the situation rather than venting and then continuing to stew over the incident. If possible, preempt the stirrings of an angry reaction by taking a time-out when you start to feel stressed. This can be just a few minutes out of your daily routine in which you spend some quiet time by yourself or take a walk.

There are numerous articles on the internet that offer techniques you can try to take your mind off anger. Keep an open mind—even if an activity seems goofy, give it a try. For example, drinking something cold or quickly doing a dozen jumping jacks distracts your body from tension. Writing about your angry feelings gives you an outlet for your anger. Counting backward from fifty distracts you from anger and refocuses your mind on something else. You might succeed in finding helpful techniques for managing your anger from unexpected sources.

CHAPTER FOUR

ANGER MANAGEMENT SKILLS FOR A HEALTHY LIFESTYLE

Successful anger management doesn't involve completely eliminating feelings of anger. Rather, it means stopping angry reactions and instead expressing anger with more constructive responses. With time, healthy anger management will become a habit that comes naturally. If you occasionally lapse back into your angry behavior, don't be discouraged. Personal change isn't easy, and slipups will happen. Ask yourself why that particular trigger set you off and analyze the feelings that could be behind your anger. Instead of reproaching yourself for failing, remind yourself of the ways in which you've improved.

SELF-AWARENESS

A primary goal of anger management is changing the angry behavior that you direct outward, but this often requires changing your inner dialogue as well. People with anger problems often focus on the negative aspects of situations. They also tend to take provocations personally and look for targets to blame. Changing these attitudes can help create a positive frame of mind that is less likely to lead to angry reactions.

Certain distorted thought patterns can predispose a person toward an angry reaction even when a situation doesn't warrant it. Some examples of distorted negative habits of thinking include:

- Assigning blame, especially when blaming a problem on the wrong source. People may turn a neutral event into a perceived offense, sometimes to avoid taking personal responsibility.

If you imagine that all your classmates dislike you just because one person said something mean to you, this is distorted negative thinking that can lead to anger without good reason.

- Assigning broad labels or viewing issues in black or white. This is the type of distorted thinking that occurs if you think, "All my classmates hate me!" just because a couple of classmates say something mean to you. A similar distortion is filtering, which is when you disregard positive aspects of a situation. If you receive mostly positive feedback on an assignment, for example, but you find yourself thinking only about a single small criticism, that's negative filtering.
- Catastrophizing or magnifying a provocation. People tend to blow things out of proportion when they're angry.
- Overgeneralizing a single provocation. If you tend to add "always" or "never" to a set of circumstances, such as, "He never keeps a promise" when a friend forgets an obligation, it can set you up for a pattern of angry reactions.

It's possible to change your thinking patterns. In psychological terms, this is called cognitive restructuring. Describe the reason you're angry and reexamine your statement.

Do the facts behind the situation justify the level of your anger? Are you using uncompromising words like "always," "never," "can't," or "must"? Take a logical rather than an emotional attitude toward the situation. Viewing the situation from the perspective of another person involved can also help you reevaluate the event.

If you conclude that there is good cause for your anger, approach the situation as a problem that needs to be solved. An angry reaction isn't constructive. Problem solving, by contrast, works toward a successful outcome. Familiarize yourself with the steps of the problem-solving process, which will include defining the problem, identifying goals, gathering ideas, developing a plan, and then executing the solution.

PRACTICING MINDFULNESS

Mindfulness can provide tools to help those struggling with problem anger change their approach. It is a mental state based in the present moment. People observe their thoughts and feelings without judging them. They don't dwell on the past or anticipate the future. Instead they maintain an awareness of their current experience.

Mindfulness techniques have proven valuable in reducing stress, and the system can also help people reexamine their anger. In his book *Calming Your Angry Mind: How Mindfulness and Compassion Can Free You from Anger and Bring Peace to Your Life*, mindfulness expert and doctor Jeffrey Brantley states, "You are not your thoughts, even when they are angry, irritated, blaming, or judging, and you do not have to be ruled by them." If you are intrigued by the idea that you can separate your sense of self from your own anger, practicing mindfulness might offer a solution for your anger issues. Try checking out websites, books, and workbooks that offer guidance on cultivating mindfulness and incorporating it into your daily life.

In some cases, old anger can persist for a long time—even going back to childhood. Unresolved anger can sometimes rankle and affect present-day attitudes. Sometimes, the best option for persistent, toxic anger is to let go and forgive past injuries for the sake of moving on.

Instead of fighting over issues such as dividing up chores, discuss the matter calmly and take responsibility for your share of the work.

GOOD COMMUNICATION

It's normal to have disagreements with your family, friends, and coworkers. This can range from banter about favorite TV shows to clashing approaches to a class project. You might feel resentment when your parents ask you to run an errand or when your friends tease you. Anger management skills can help you prevent yourself from losing your temper at such provocations, but it's not healthy to suppress the feelings behind your anger either.

Consider whether you need to improve your communication skills. People with anger management problems tend to turn interactions into confrontations. A healthy alternative is assertive communication, in which people express opinions calmly and respectfully.

Anger management experts often recommend that assertive communication statements focus on facts, feelings, and fair requests (the "three F's"). The goal should be to share feelings and open a discussion about a situation. Avoid some of the pitfalls of an aggressive confrontation, such as trying to dominate the conversation, blaming, judging, or insulting the other person or defensively shutting down the discussion. At the same time, you should resist being too passive and failing to share your needs. Being respectful during a discussion doesn't mean that you have to tolerate mistreatment.

During the discussion, avoid escalating it into an argument. Instead, negotiate over points of disagreement and attempt to reach a compromise acceptable to everyone. If you feel yourself starting to lose control, speak quietly and slowly. If you find yourself making demands of the other person, reframe them as requests.

Improving your listening skills can also improve your communication with other people. People tend to rush to conclusions when they're angry, often failing to heed the message the other person is trying to convey. Before responding, think over whether you appreciate the other person's concerns. In a process called active listening, one person paraphrases the other's statement when they're done speaking and sometimes offers an interpretation of their perspective. This exercise can help communication and clear up misunderstandings.

Many experts recommend using "I" statements that convey your position rather than "you" statements that tend to place blame. For example, instead of saying, "You're being too demanding," reframe your message as, "I'm having trouble handling so many responsibilities." This approach can prevent tension from escalating.

As you work on managing your anger and improving communication, share your goals with your family and friends and ask for their support. Let them know that they can count on you for support with their problems as well.

Teens may feel pressure from parents and teachers to do well in school, sports, and other extracurricular activities. It can be stressful.

MANAGING STRESS

Many high school students report experiencing high levels of stress in their daily lives. They feel under

A balanced diet is essential for adolescents, and taking time to enjoy a good healthy meal can provide an opportunity to unwind from the stress of daily life.

pressure from the demands of school, extracurricular activities, family, and work. They worry about money, grades, health, relationships, and current events. Even during leisure time, keeping up with social media sometimes prevents kids from fully relaxing.

Stress can make anger management more difficult. Stress affects both the body and mind, producing physical effects, such as tenseness or headaches, along with psychological effects, such as anxiety or irritability. People feel unsettled and overwhelmed when they're under stress, and they're much more likely to react angrily to minor triggers.

Managing stress is an important life skill for any teenager. Take stock of the factors in your life that make you feel stressed. These include both minor irritants of everyday life as well as major crises that occur less frequently. Once you've identified the most pressing sources of stress in your life, come up with tactics for coping. In addition, try adjusting your expectations and maintaining a sense of perspective, especially concerning school and grades.

A healthy lifestyle is important for managing stress and overall well-being. Make sure that you eat a nutritious diet that includes regular meals and minimizes junk food. Get plenty of sleep, which will help you function better throughout the day. Exercise helps reduce feelings of stress and provides many other health benefits, both physical and mental. Make time in your schedule to relax with activities you enjoy, and be sure to spend quality time with family and friends.

CHAPTER FIVE

GETTING HELP

For some people, self-help strategies aren't enough to resolve an anger management problem. If problem anger starts negatively affecting your behavior at home, school, or work, you should consider a structured anger management program or treatment with a mental health professional.

People suffering from mental health or emotional issues are sometimes reluctant to get help. They're afraid that it might be seen as a personal failing. Remember that addressing anger management problems early in your life will improve your future personal relationships, job prospects, and overall well-being. If professional help isn't readily available to you, research further resources online and at your library, health centers, and school. A trusted teacher or counselor might be able to give you advice.

ANGER MANAGEMENT CLASSES

Anger management classes are a standard option for people seeking help for problem anger. Studies of anger management programs, such as a 2003 analysis by psychologists Raymond DiGiuseppe and Raymond Chip Tafrate, have found them to be successful in helping people change their behavior. Anger management classes are often mandated after public outbursts. In these cases, completion is required by a school or employer, or by a court of law. A typical class lasts for about eight or ten weeks. There are many different formats for anger management classes, and they can be offered by health care providers, religious organizations, and community groups. Some programs are tailored specifically to children and teens.

Trained counselors and therapists can help people address the thoughts, reactions, and behaviors related to toxic anger. They're experienced in helping people gain control of problem anger.

Anger management classes generally emphasize many of the standard means of controlling anger discussed in self-help books and websites. The process often begins with an assessment of the person's personal anger profile, which examines qualities such as communication skills, stress, and empathy, as well as how the person handles anger. During the classes, people begin by identifying their triggers and symptoms of anger, both mental and physical. They learn new behaviors, ways of thinking, and communication skills to help them cope with anger. The end goal is to improve how well people control their anger and communicate assertively. Anger management classes

Group therapy sessions give people the opportunity to recognize they're not alone in their struggles and to give and receive support from others.

aim to forestall some of the most extreme consequences of problem anger, such as health problems, psychological issues, problems with relationships, trouble at work, and substance abuse.

Courses may involve group classes as well as one-on-one sessions. Attendees often find that the structured format helps them maintain their focus on changing their behavior. Group support can also be very helpful for some people. Attendees share stories about their individual circumstances and offer feedback. They may enact role-playing scenarios, in which attendees practice constructive responses in provocative situations and receive feedback. Participating in a group setting can help with the goal of improving communication and empathy for others.

SIGNING UP FOR THERAPY

Another treatment for anger management is therapy with a psychologist or psychiatrist. This can be particularly helpful for people who are addressing mental health issues in addition to anger management, but anyone with anger problems can benefit from therapy. Psychologists are highly educated health professionals experienced in treating people with mental health issues. Some psychologists specialize in treating children and teenagers. To find a qualified psychologist, ask your primary health care provider to recommend someone or search online through reputable sites such as professional associations. It's important that a patient be able to establish a trusting relationship with a psychologist. If you're having a bad experience with a therapist, consider consulting someone else.

One of the most commonly used types of therapy is called cognitive behavioral therapy (CBT). In CBT, patients examine the thought processes that are contributing to an emotional problem. They learn to disrupt negative thought patterns and replace them with more constructive alternatives. Patients also address their behavior by changing reactions to the sources of their emotional issues. For people dealing with problem anger, this means the triggers for outbursts. The therapist will help them examine the reasons behind their prob-

Overcoming problem anger can improve a person's communication skills, relationships with others, and overall satisfaction at school, at home, and beyond.

lem. They learn ways of asserting themselves without aggression and deescalating anger during tense situations.

Cognitive behavioral therapy is a goal-oriented treatment. Patients should expect homework, such as keeping logs and completing reading assignments. Treatment length varies depending on an individual's circumstances, but ten to twenty sessions is typical for dealing with anger management issues.

INTERMITTENT EXPLOSIVE DISORDER

The mental health condition known as intermittent explosive disorder (IED) is marked by aggressive and destructive anger. People diagnosed with IED are prone to erupting into impulsive rages that are out of proportion to the provocation, with no regard for the consequences of their actions. They often behave in violent and frightening ways. Road rage, assaults, and property destruction sometimes result from an outburst. The consequences of IED can include school suspension, problems with relationships, job loss, and legal troubles.

Symptoms of IED usually begin in childhood or adolescence, and most people diagnosed are male. The condition is often linked to depression, anxiety, and substance abuse disorders occurring later in life. Treatment of IED may involve medication, therapy, and anger management techniques such as cognitive restructuring and relaxation techniques.

Psychiatrists are doctors who specialize in treating mental health issues. Anger is not an official mental disorder, so people with anger management issues should not expect to be prescribed medications to treat problem anger. For patients dealing with related mental health problems such as depression, however, medications such as antidepressants may also help with managing anger.

LOOKING FORWARD

Successful anger management is a valuable skill for a promising future. After you're done with high school, you'll undertake a new set of opportunities that will provide new challenges, stresses, and frustrations. If you've learned some anger management techniques, you'll be equipped to deal with these challenges without resorting to angry reactions when things are difficult. The tools and habits that keep anger under control will also prove valuable in other areas of your life. Relaxation techniques are useful for managing stress. Good communication skills are essential for healthy relationships and success on the job. Self-awareness and making time for leisure activities will help maintain your physical and mental well-being.

10 GREAT QUESTIONS TO ASK A COUNSELOR

1. What are some of the signs that someone has a problem with anger management?
2. What are some of the causes of problem anger?
3. What tactics can I use in dealing with a friend or family member who has an anger management problem?
4. How can I prevent myself from reacting angrily to a specific trigger?
5. What are some good ways to cool down when I find myself starting to feel angry?
6. What relaxation techniques can I use to help deal with anger?
7. How can I communicate assertively during a tense situation without becoming overly aggressive or demanding?
8. Can you recommend an anger management workbook that can provide tools for anger management?
9. Are there any support groups, mental health centers, or social service agencies in my community that provide anger management resources?
10. How do I find a mental health professional who can help me with anger management issues?

GLOSSARY

adolescence The period of growth and development during which a child matures into an adult.

aggression Hostile or destructive behavior, often intended to harm another.

anxiety An emotion characterized by feelings of tension, worried thoughts, and physical changes like increased blood pressure.

assertive Confident and direct in expressing one's views.

chronic Continuing for a long time or frequently recurring.

cognitive behavioral therapy (CBT) A type of therapy that helps people suffering from mental health issues change their thinking patterns and behaviors.

confrontation A hostile or contentious situation, especially between two or more parties.

depression A mental illness in which feelings of sadness, loss, anger, or frustration interfere with everyday life for an extended period of time.

emotion A feeling or state of mind.

excessive Going beyond what is necessary.

express To convey through words or other means of communication.

frustration A state of being annoyed or dissatisfied, especially because of an unresolved problem or a failure to achieve something.

impulsive Acting without thought or planning.

intense Strong or extreme.

passive-aggressive Characterizing a personality that tends to express negative emotions through indirect means.

perspective A point of view or way of regarding a situation.

provoke To enrage or arouse a reaction.

reaction A feeling or behavior that results because of a situation, influence, or event.

relapse To return or slip back to a previous state or behavior.

strategy An action plan intended to achieve a goal, especially a long-term one.

stress Strain or tension involving mental, emotional, and physical responses.

tactic A plan or method intended to achieve a result.

therapy The treatment of mental health problems using psychological means.

vent To express or release strong emotions.

FOR MORE INFORMATION

American Psychological Association (APA)
750 First Street NE
Washington, DC 20002
(800) 374-2721
Website: http://www.apa.org
Facebook: @AmericanPsychologicalAssociation
Twitter: @apa
The APA is a scientific and professional organization that represents psychologists in the United States. It also provides education about psychology, behavioral science, and mental health.

Canadian Mental Health Association (CMHA)
1110-151 Slater Street
Ottawa, ON K1P 5H3
Canada
Website: http://www.cmha.ca
Facebook and Instagram: @CMHANational
Twitter: @CMHA_NTL
The Canadian Mental Health Association (CMHA) promotes the mental health of all and supports the resilience and recovery of people experiencing mental illness.

Health Canada
Address Locator 0900C2
Ottawa, ON K1A 0K9
Canada

(613) 957-2991
Website: https://www.canada.ca/en/health-canada.html
Facebook: @HealthyCdns, @HealthyFirstNationsandInuit
Twitter: @GovCanHealth
A federal institution of the government of Canada, Health Canada provides services to help Canadians maintain and improve health.

Mental Health America (MHA)
500 Montgomery Street, Suite 820
Alexandria, VA 22314
(703) 684-7722
Website: http://www.MentalHealthAmerica.net
Facebook, Instagram, and Twitter: @mentalhealthamerica
MHA is a community-based nonprofit dedicated to addressing the needs of those living with mental illness and promoting the overall mental health of all Americans.

National Institute of Mental Health (NIMH)
Science Writing, Press, and Dissemination Branch
6001 Executive Boulevard, Room 6200, MSC 9663
Bethesda, MD 20892
(866) 615-6464
Website: http://www.nimh.nih.gov
Facebook and Twitter: @nimhgov
The mission of the NIMH is to transform the understanding and treatment of mental illnesses through basic and clinical research, paving the way for prevention, recovery, and cure.

Psych Central
55 Pleasant Street, Suite 207
Newburyport, MA 01950
Website: http://PsychCentral.com
Twitter: @PsychCentral
Psych Central is a mental health resource that provides mental health information, emotional support, and advocacy.

US Department of Health & Human Services
Office of Adolescent Health (OAH)
1101 Wootton Parkway, Suite 700
Rockville, MD 20852
(240) 453-2846
Website: https://www.hhs.gov/ash/oah
Twitter: @TeenHealthGov
The OAH is dedicated to improving the health and well-being of adolescents. It provides information about important mental health habits in the "Mental Health" section of its website.

FOR FURTHER READING

Alvord, Mary Karapetian, and Anne McGrath. *Conquer Negative Thinking for Teens: A Workbook to Break the Nine Thought Habits That Are Holding You Back.* Oakland, CA: Instant Help Books, 2017.

Brantley, Jeffrey. *Calming Your Angry Mind: How Mindfulness and Compassion Can Free You from Anger and Bring Peace to Your Life.* Oakland, CA: New Harbinger Publications, 2014.

Covey, Sean. *The 6 Most Important Decisions You'll Ever Make: A Guide for Teens: Updated for the Digital Age.* New York, NY: Touchstone, 2017.

Donovan, Sandra. *Communication Smarts: How to Express Yourself Best in Conversations, Texts, E-mails, and More.* Minneapolis, MN: Twenty-First Century Books, 2013.

Elliott, Charles H., and Laura L. Smith. *Anger Management for Dummies.* 2nd ed. Hoboken, NJ: John Wiley & Sons, Inc., 2015.

Lohmann, Raychelle Cassada. *The Anger Workbook for Teens: Activities to Help You Deal with Anger and Frustration.* Oakland, CA: Instant Help Books, 2009.

Puff, Robert. *The Everything Guide to Anger Management.* Avon, MA: Adams Media, 2014.

Skeen, Michelle. *Communication Skills for Teens: How to Listen, Express & Connect for Success.*

Oakland, CA: Instant Help Books, 2016.
Stebner, Beth. *Stop, Breathe, Chill: Meditations for A Less Stressful, More Awesome Life.* Avon, MA: Adams Media, 2016.
Van Dijk, Sheri. *Surviving the Emotional Roller Coaster: DBT Skills to Help Teens Manage Emotions.* Oakland, CA: Instant Help Books, 2016.
Waters, Rosa. *Anger*. Broomall, PA: Mason Crest, 2015.
Wroble, Lisa A. *Dealing with Stress: A How-to Guide.* Berkeley Heights, NJ: Enslow Publishers, Inc., 2012.

BIBLIOGRAPHY

American Psychological Association. "Controlling anger before it controls you." Retrieved February 1, 2018. http://www.apa.org/topics/anger/control.aspx.

American Psychological Association. "Tips for Managing Anger." Retrieved February 1, 2018 https://psychcentral.com/lib/tips-for-managing-anger.

Brantley, Jeffrey. *Calming Your Angry Mind: How Mindfulness and Compassion Can Free You from Anger and Bring Peace to Your Life.* Oakland, CA: New Harbinger Publications, 2014.

CBS Chicago. "'Disruptive' Woman Removed From Flight To Chicago." July 6, 2017. http://chicago.cbslocal.com/2017/07/06/american-airlines-disruptive-passenger-removed.

Dean, Jeremy. "The Upside of Anger: 6 Psychological Benefits of Getting Mad." PsyBlog, March 6, 2012. http://www.spring.org.uk/2012/03/the-upside-of-anger-6-psychological-benefits-of-getting-mad.php.

DiGiuseppe, Raymond, and Raymond Chip Tafrate. "Anger Treatment for Adults: A Meta-Analysic Review." *Clinical Psychology: Science and Practice*, March 2003. http://onlinelibrary.wiley.com=/doi/10.1093/clipsy.10.1.70/abstract.

Elliott, Charles H., and Laura L. Smith. *Anger Management for Dummies.* 2nd ed. Hoboken, NJ: John Wiley & Sons, Inc., 2015.

Golden, Bernard. *Overcoming Destructive Anger: Strategies That Work.* Baltimore, MD: Johns Hopkins University Press, 2016.

Hammond, Christine. "19 Things to Do with Anger Other Than Explode." Psych Central, December 29, 2017. https://pro.psychcentral.com/exhausted-woman/2017/12/19-things-to-do-with-anger-other-than-explode.

James, Matt. "React vs Respond What's the Difference?" *Psychology Today*, September 1, 2016. https://www.psychologytoday.com/blog/focus-forgiveness/201609/react-vs-respond.

Mayo Clinic. "Anger Management." June 10, 2017. https://www.mayoclinic.org/tests-procedures/anger-management/about/pac-20385186.

McCarthy, Eliza. "Using Anger-Management Techniques to Cope with 2017." The Cut, November 22, 2017. https://www.thecut.com/2017/11/using-anger-management-techniques-to-cope-with-2017.html.

McCay, Mathew, and Peter Rogers. *The Anger Control Workbook: Simple, Innovative Techniques for Managing Anger and Developing Healthier Ways of Relating.* Oakland, CA: New Harbinger Publications, 2000.

Potter-Efron, Ronald T. *Angry All the Time: An Emergency Guide to Anger Control.* 2nd ed. Oakland, CA: New Harbinger Publications, Inc., 2004.

Potter-Efron, Ronald T. *Letting Go of Anger: The Eleven Most Common Anger Styles and What to Do About Them.* 2nd ed. Oakland, CA: New Harbinger Publications, Inc., 2006.

Potter-Efron, Ronald T. *Rage: A Step-by-Step Guide to Overcoming Explosive Anger.* Oakland, CA: New Harbinger Publications, Inc., 2007.

Psychology Today. "Intermittent Explosive Disorder." June 14, 2017. https://www.psychologytoday.com/conditions/intermittent-explosive-disorder.

Richardson, Celia, and Ed Halliwell. "Boiling Point: Problem Anger and What We Can Do About It." Mental Health Foundation, 2008. https://www.mentalhealth.org.uk/sites/default/files/boilingpoint.pdf.

Segal, Jeanne, and Melinda Smith. "Anger Management: Tips and Techniques for Getting Anger Under Control." Helpguide.org. Retrieved February 1, 2018. https://www.helpguide.org/articles/relationships-communication/anger-management.htm.

Svitil, Kathy A. *Calming the Anger Storm.* New York, NY: Alpha Books, 2005.

WedMD. "Mental Health and Anger Management." September 21, 2016. https://www.webmd.com/mental-health/anger-management.

INDEX

ABOUT THE AUTHOR

Corona Brezina is an author who has written numerous young adult books for Rosen Publishing. Several of her previous books have focused on legal and social issues concerning teens, including *Personal Freedom and Civic Duty: Understanding Equal Rights* and *Standing Up to Bullying at School*. She lives in Chicago.

PHOTO CREDITS

Cover crazystocker/Shutterstock.com; back cover Photo by Marianna armata/Moment/Getty Images; p. 5 Stuart Jenner/Shutterstock.com; pp. 7, 17, 26, 35, 44 markmandersonfilms/Shutterstock.com; p. 8 anyaberkut/iStock/Thinkstock; p. 11 a katz/Shutterstock.com; p. 14 pixelheadphoto digitalskillet/Shutterstock.com; p. 18 imtmphoto/iStock/Thinkstock; p. 19 Rocketclips, Inc./Shutterstock.com; p. 21 Naked King/iStock/Thinkstock; p. 25 susan.k./Moment/Getty Images; p. 27 SiraFilm/Shutterstock.com; p. 30 maxpetrov/Shutterstock.com; p. 32 Kosim Shukurov/Shutterstock.com; p. 34 Martin Barraud/The Image Bank/Getty Images; pp. 36, 45 fstop123/E+/Getty Images; p. 39 Yellow Dog Productions/The Image Bank/Getty Images; p. 41 Randy Faris/Corbis/Getty Images; p. 42 James Tse/Photographer's Choice/Getty Images; p. 46 Martin Barraud/Calaimage/Getty Images; p. 48 Klaus Vedfelt/DigitalVision/Getty Images.

Design: Michael Moy; Layout and Photo Research: Ellina Litmanovich; Editor: Rachel Aimee